The Poetry of Bliss Carman

Volume XV - Pipes of Pan No V. From the Book of Valentines

William Bliss Carman was born in Fredericton, in New Brunswick on April 15th 1861. He was educated at Fredericton Collegiate School before moving to the University of New Brunswick, obtaining his B.A. there in 1881. As is common with so many writers his first published piece was for the University magazine and for Carman that was in 1879.

After several years editing various magazines and periodicals Carman first published a poetry volume in 1893 with Low Tide on Grand Pré. There was no Canadian company prepared to publish and when an American company did so it went bankrupt.

The following year was decidedly better. His partnership with the American poet Richard Hovey had given birth to Songs of Vagabondia. It was an immediate success.

That success prompted the Boston firm, Stone & Kimball, to reissue Low Tide on Grand Pré and to hire Carman as the editor of its literary journal, The Chapbook.

Carman brought out, in 1895, Behind the Arras, a somewhat more serious and philosophical work centered on the premise of a long meditation, using the speaker's house and its many rooms, as a symbol of life and the choices to be made.

In 1896 Carman met Mrs Mary Perry King, who rapidly became patron, adviser and sometime lover. She also became his writing collaborator on two verse dramas.

In 1897 Carman published Ballad of Lost Haven, and in 1898, By the Aurelian Wall, the title poem itself was an elegy to John Keats and the book was a collection of formal elegies.

As the century turned Carman was hard at work on a five-volume set of poetry "Pans Pipes". The excellence of a number of these poems did much to install Carman as the most noted of Canadian Poets and eventually their own Poet Laureate.

In 1912 the final work in the Vagabondia series was published. Richard Hovey had died in 1900 and so this last work was purely Carman's. It has a distinct elegiac tone as if remembering the past works themselves.

On October 28th, 1921 Carman was honored by the newly-formed Canadian Authors' Association where he was crowned Canada's Poet Laureate with a wreath of maple leaves.

William Bliss Carman died of a brain hemorrhage at the age of 68 in New Canaan on the 8th June, 1929.

Index of Contents

BALLAD OF THE YOUNG KING'S MADNESS

In a Kingdom long ago, as the story comes to me,
There lived a sturdy folk by the borders of the sea;
The snow-tipped mountains behind them guarding the East and the North,
While open to Southward and Westward, were the sea-gates bidding them forth.

Launching their boats through the breakers, casting their nets in the tide,
The sea had given them daring, strength and endurance and pride;
Watching their sheep with the eagles on many a lonely hill,
The stars had given them knowledge and insight and ghostly skill;

For wisdom comes to the waiting as water comes to a mill,
From unsluiced sources of silence where the chatter of life grows still.

I.

Over this sturdy people there ruled without favour or greed
A man with the arm and heart of the olden kingly breed.
There was never a sport nor contest, there was never a horse to tame,
But the King would meet all comers, and was ever first in the game.

A speaker of truth to all men, he carried his will with a word;
And Justice dwelt in his borders, nor ever un-sheathed her sword.
Likable, open and reckless, he neither bullied nor feared,
When over the rim of his empire threatening danger appeared,
But in the face of his council laughed in his yellow beard.

Yet his light-heart ways were a scandal to the seemly and the sage,
He would turn from the weightiest business to rally a love-sick page,
Twitting him for a laggard, making him blush with a jest,
Shaming him for a waster by the good wine spilt on his vest.

Never a band of minstrels passed, but he bade them in,
Haling the lads by the shoulder, taking the maids by the chin;
Till the courtyard gleamed with motley, and the palace rang with din.

Courtiers lived on his bounty, lights-of-love supped at his board.
Merry the time he gave them, priceless the wine he poured,
Lavish of all his substance for the gay and careless horde;
Till long lips groaning abhorrence had evil things to foretell.
But always the children loved him, and the women passing well.

II.

So time wore on, and the King awoke one day with a start,
To hear a strange new whisper of discontent in his heart.
Pleasure he had in plenty, health, and companions, and power;
Yet what is all this life but a void and empty hour?

Fair was the golden morning with April over the hill.
He strolled to the gate of the palace and stood there grave and still,
Watching the mountain shadows, then shut his teeth on his will.
"Bring me a horse," he ordered. They saddled his favourite bay;
And down through the watered valley the young King rode away;
Down through the flowery orchards, where the river babbles and shines,
Past ford and smithy and farm, and up where the narrowing lines
Of tillage and pasture vanish in the dusk of the purple pines.
How speculation and rumour fluttered his folk that day!
"Who can fathom his fancies? Mad as a hare!" said they.

In a cleft of the solemn mountains, like a thought in earth's green heart,
Stood a hospice of recluse men, quiet, secluded, apart,
Having forgotten the world and left distraction behind,
For care of the troublous want and hunger of the mind.

There as the night was falling, the King on his red mare came,
And they have welcomed the stranger, asking not station nor name.
Who bides at the house of God needs neither money nor fame.

Never an eyelid flickered, never a word betrayed
They knew the habit and bearing accustomed to be obeyed;
But after the rule of their order, equal in everything,
With kingly love for a brother the brothers served their King.

They gave him his seat at table, cell and habit and stall.
The scanty fare and the hours of prayer, meekly he took them all;
Nor ever they found him wanting in duties great or small.

Lowly he sat before them and many a lecture heard,
Questioned and reasoned and listened, argued, proved and conferred,
And by many a lonely candle pondered the printed word.

Daily the power of knowledge grew and spread in his face;
Daily the look of the scholar glowed with a finer trace;
Daily the tan-flush faded and ever he grew in grace,
As understanding within him climbed to her lawful place.

So from the man of sinew they made a student at last,
Thoughtful and grave as he had been brave; till, lo, three years had passed,
And the young King yawned one day, stretching himself in the sun,
And murmured: "Now let's see what their book-learning has done!
The arms grow feeble, alack! The foot and eye grow slow;
Let's put their lore to the test. Good friends, this day I go."

So said, so done. Mused the Brothers, watching him down the hill:
"Feeble must be our virtue, if this hope comes to ill."
They saw him lost in dust; and the sundown's dying rose
Kindled their lofty hill-crest in its eternal snows.

III.

Now well the Kingdom prospered while the young King was away,
For wise were the heads of his council, leaders of men in their day,
Stubborn at fronting clamour, strong to govern and sway,
Of tested honour and flawless tried in the world's assay.

Yet there was joy at his coming, throngs that laughed with delight,
Cheers as he passed and waving, children held in his sight,
Flags hung out at the windows, and bonfires lit in the night.
Comrades met on the corner, cronies talked in the door,
"The merry times are returning; we shall have revels once more."

But they reckoned without their host, if they thought the glorious days
Of the King's wild youth had returned with their drinking and masques and plays.
Sober he sat at council, wisely he judged and decreed,

Till the frivolous gaped and muttered: "A paragon indeed!"

Tireless, toiling and thoughtful, steadfast, kingly and tall,
But lonely he lived, unloving, blameless before them all,
With never a rose in his bower nor a bosom-friend in his hall.

And ever his brow grew whiter, his eye more hungry bright,
For the blessing of peace escaped him, though he toiled by day and night.
By lamplight and daylight he laboured, till his visage grew lean and grim,
While his people saw and wondered, and their hearts went out to him.

So he strove for a year or more, and never was seen to fail
In the least or the greatest matter where diligence might avail.
Yet ever he grew more restless, and ever his cheek more pale.

IV.

Now it chanced on another morning like that when he rode away,
The King must come to his seaboard, where a foreign galleon lay,
Black hull and gleaming canvas, with her decks in trim array;
Long and graceful and speedy as a flying fish was she,
Showing the scarlet pennon of the gypsies of the sea.

There in a dream he stood; watching the surf and the sand;
Then all of a sudden he laughed, as the rowers rowed to land.
"God of my fathers," he cried. " What manner of fool am I?
A landsman all my life, a sea-king will I die."

Needs must they humour him then, whispering, "Mad once more!"
As they heard him speak to the sailors, and saw him rowed from the shore.
Small room to parley or caution, and smaller use to deplore;
When a strong man comes to his stronghold, fate must yield him the door.

Lightly he stood in the boat, when the bending rowers rowed;
And the wind and the tide and the sun freshened and sparkled and glowed.
There lay the sea before him fair as an open road.

Last they saw of the King was at the helmsman's side,
Gay in the light of adventure, while the vessel swung on the tide.
With a song they hove her anchor; the sails drew taut and free;
And she heeled to the wind and lessened on the long blue slope of the sea.

V.

The sun came up, the sun went down, the tide drew out and in,
But never a word that seaport heard from foreigner or kin,

Rower, merchant, or sailorman, or the gypsies of the sea,

Whither their prince had vanished, or what his fate might be;
Till a thousand suns had circled, and twice a thousand tides
Had swung the swaying harbour buoys and brimmed through the channel guides.

Then through a winter twilight when the sun was a disk of red,
The keen-eyed watcher beheld, as he gazed from the harbour-head,
A moving speck like a seahawk crossing that targe of flame;
And beating up from the sea-rim the gypsy galleon came.

And why is she decked with pennons, and trimmed with cloth of gold?
And what are these scarlet trappings the harbour folk behold?
What means her glory of banners fluttering on the breeze,
Brave as the coloured autumn that is the pride of the trees?
Has she rifled a sea-king's treasure and plundered the isles of the seas?

Slowly she passed the entry, the white sails lowered and furled,
And there was our long-lost truant from the other side of the world.
On the deck he stood, the figure of a man to make men bold,
A browned and hardy master, as debonair as of old,
The strength of his hands as aforetime, the scholar's light on his brow,
But something passing knowledge in his look and bearing now,

The calm of a radiant purpose, the joy of unerring quest,
The poise of perfected being when the soul attains her best.
He had ruled with power and pleasure, he had searched and found out lore;
And now his unfainting spirit had discovered the one thing more.

But the curious eye forsook him to greet with amazed regard
Another who stood at the taffrail by the sheet of the great main-yard;
Fine as a mast in stature, eager, unflinching, and free,
With hair like the sun's raw gold and eyes like crumbs of the sea;
Straight-browed — the imperial bearing of one who is born to sway,

Deep-bosomed with all the ardour that kindles our wondrous clay;
Regent of glad dominions, a sea-trove out of the vast
Wide welter of life. "A hostage fit for our king at last!"

Threefold is the search for perfection that leads through creation's plan
Through immemorial nature and the restless heart of man;
Beauty of shape and colour to gladden and profit the eye,
Truth beyond cavil or question to answer the reason why,
And the blameless spirit's portion the joy that shall not die.

The dauntless soul must wander to accomplish and attain
This balance of all her powers by the lead of love, or remain
A stranger to peace forever in sorrow, defeat, and pain.

Flushed with the cheers of welcome, lightly the king, all pride,
Handed the girl, all beauty, over the vessel's side.
Then in a lull of their salvos, to the wondering crowd that rings
The pierhead, eager to question, "Our queen," said the sanest of kings.

ACROSS THE COURTYARD

That is the window over there
With the closed shutters and the air
Of a deserted place, like those
Abandoned homesteads whose repose
Haunts us with mystery. Inside
Who knows what tragedy may hide?

This window has been sealed up so
A fortnight now. A month ago
Just about dusk you should have seen
The vision I saw smile and lean
From that same window. Spring's return,
When daffodils and jonquils burn
Under the azure April day,
Is not more lovely nor more gay.
The world at least, our artist world
Where tubes are pinched and brushes twirled
In the long task to reproduce
God's masterpieces for man's use
Knows Jacynth for the loveliest
Of all its models and the best.
Why, half the portraits in the town,
From Mrs. Bigwig, Jr.'s down,
Have that same perfect taper hand.
(If you have wit to understand
A woman's vanity, you know
Why they should wish to have it so),
Those same long fingers smooth and round,
Faultless as petals, and not found
Twice in a generation. Well,
They're Jacynth's. But you need not tell
The trick. In this world art must live
On what the world's caprice will give.

Delightful folly! But far more
Delightful beauty we adore
And follow humbly day by day,
Her difficult, enchanted way.

(Dear beauty, still beyond the reach
Of paint, or music, or of speech!)
We toil and triumph and despair,
Then on a morn look up, and there
Some girl goes by, or there's a dash
Of colour on the clouds — a flash
Of inspiration caught between
Chinks in the workshop's grey routine.
One hint of glory through the murk,
And God has criticized our work.

So we plod on, and so one day
It happened toward the end of May,
When the long twilight comes, and when
Our northern orchards bloom again
Even our poor old courtyard tree,
Knowing the time that bids him be
One of the hosts that leaf and sing
In the revival of the spring,
Dons his green robe of joy. You know
How idle, then, a man will grow.
I had been sitting lost in thought
Of how our best dreams come to naught,
And we are left mere daubers still
For want of knowledge, lack of skill —
So many of us are, I mean!
The door was open, and the screen
And curtains turned back everywhere
For the first breath of summer air,
That came in like a wanderer
From far untroubled lands, to stir
The prints along the wall, and bring
Our dreams of greatness back with spring.

Suddenly, I looked up, aware
Before I looked, of some one there —
You know how. In the doorway stood
A tall girl dressed in black. How good
A scrap of actual beauty is,
After our unrealities!
The copper-coloured hair; the glint
Of tea-rose in her throat's warm tint;
The magic and surprise that go
With level blue-grey eyes; the slow
Luxurious charm of poise and line,
Half-Oriental, half-divine,
And altogether human. Oh,
One must have known her then, to know

How faultless beauty still transcends
The bound where faultless painting ends.
But you may gather here and there
Faint glimpses and reports of her
In the best work of all the men
Who painted her as she was then,
Splendid and wonderful. To me,
For colour and for symmetry,
In her young glory there she seemed
The flame-like one of whom they dreamed
Who worshipped beauty in old days
With singleness of joy and praise;
Some great Astarte come to bless
This old world with new loveliness;
My own ideal come to life,
After the failure and the strife,
To prove I dreamed not all in vain
In poverty beside the Seine.

There came a sudden leap at heart
That made my pulses stop and start,
The surge and flood of sense that sweep
Over our nature's hidden deep,
When we look up and recognize
Our vision in an earthly guise.
Then reason must resign control
To the indubitable soul,
Put off despair, arise and dance
To the joy-music of romance.

For one great year she posed for me;
Came in and out familiarly,
And made the studio her home
Almost not quite; for always some
What shall I say? reserve or pride,
Mysterious and aloof, belied
By the soft loving languorous mien,
Invested her, enthroned serene
Above importunings. Who knows,
If she had chosen as I chose
Flung heart and head and hand away
On the great venture of a day;
Poured love and passion and romance
In the frail mould of circumstance
Had she but dared be one of two,
We might have made the world anew!
However much it might have cost,
Who knows what good may have been lost,

What passing great reward?

One day
When work was done she turned to say
Her soft good night, and tripped down-stair
With rustling skirts and her fine air
Of breeziness, humming a catch
From some street-song. I heard the latch
Click after her, and she was gone.
Next day I waited. It wore on
To afternoon, and still no sign
Of peril near this dream of mine.
A year went by, and not a word
Of the lost Jacynth could be heard.

May came again; the wind once more
Was blowing by the open door,
And I saw something over there
Across the yard that made me stare.

Strangers had recently arrived
On that third floor, and Fate contrived
One of her small dramatic scenes
Which make us wonder what life means,
And whether it is all a play
For our diversion by the way.
There at the window I caught sight
Of a girl's figure. The crisp white
Of the fresh gown passed and repassed,
Strangely familiar, till at last,
"Jacynth, of course! Who else?" I cried.
And on the instant she espied
Me watching her; quick as a flash
And smiling, ran, threw up the sash
To lean far out. "How do you do,
My friend?" "Why, Jacynth, how are you,
After this long, long time? " I said.
"Thank you, quite well." Her pretty head
Was tilted up, in every line
An old medallion rare and fine.

"Yes, it's a long time, isn't it,
Since that first day I came to sit
For your great Lilith? Tell me how
They hung it at the Fair. And now
That we are neighbours once again,
Do come to see me." It was plain
From the unwonted vanity

Of tone, as she ran on to me,
Some strange ambition, plan, or hope
Had come to give her pride new scope.
Somehow she had acquired the chill
Of worldliness; I missed the thrill
Of eager radiance she had
When we were comrades free and glad.
Some volatile and subtle trace
Of soul had vanished from her face,
Leaving the brilliancy that springs
From polished and enamelled things.
The beauty of the lamp still shone
With lustre, but the flame was gone.

There was so evident in her
The smug complacent character
Of prosperous security,
That when, with just a flick at me,
She added, gaily as before,
"It isn't Jacynth any more,
It's Mrs. "some one here was I,
Too much astonished to reply,
Before she vanished. From that day
The rest is blank, think what you may.
There is her window, as you see,
Closed on a teasing mystery.

I think, as I recall her here,
How much life means beyond the mere
Safety, convenience, and the pose
Respectability bestows;
The beauty of the questing soul
In every face, beyond control
Is dimmed by wearing any mask
That dull conformity may ask.
How almost no one understands
The unworldliness that art demands!
How few have courage to retain
Through years of doubtful stress and strain
The resolute and lonely will
To follow beauty, to fulfil
The dreams of their prophetic youth
And pay the utmost price of truth!
How few have nerve enough to keep
The trail, and thread the dark and steep
By the lone lightning-flash that falls
Through sullen murky intervals!
How many faint of heart must choose

The steady lantern for their use,
And never, without fear of Fate,
Be daring, generous arid great!

Where is she now? What sudden change
Clouded our day-dream? Love is strange!

A NEIGHBOUR'S CREED

" Nor knowest thou what argument
Thy life to thy neighbour's creed has lent?

I.

All day the weary crowds move on
Through the grey city's stifling heat,
With anxious air, with jaded mien,
To strife, to labour, to defeat.

But I possess my soul in calm,
Because I know, unvexed by noise,
Somewhere across the city's hum
Your splendid spirit keeps its poise.

II.

Because I see you bright and brave,
I say to my despondent heart,
"Up, loiterer! Put off this guise
Of gloom, and play the sturdier part!"

Three things are given man to do:
To dare, to labour, and to grow.
Not otherwise from earth we came,
Nor otherwise our way we go.

Three things are given man to be:
Cheerful, undoubting, and humane,
Surviving through the direst fray,
Preserving the untarnished strain.

Three things are given man to know:
Beauty and truth and honour. These
Are the nine virtues of the soul,
Her mystic powers and ecstasies.

And when I see you bravely tread
That difficult and doubtful way,
"Up, waverer; wilt thou forsake
Thy comrade? "to my soul I say.

Then bitterness and sullen fear,
Mistrust and anger, are no more.
That quick gay step is in the hall;
That rallying voice is at the door.

TO ONE IN DESPAIR

I.

O die not yet, great heart; but deign
A little longer to endure
This life of passionate fret and strain,
Of slender hope and joy unsure!

Take Contemplation by the sleeve,
And ask her, " Is it not worth while
To teach my fellows not to grieve, —
To lend them courage in a smile?

"Is it so little to have made
The timorous ashamed of fear, —
The idle and the false afraid
To front existence with a sneer?"

For those who live within your sway
Know not a mortal fear, save one,
That some irreparable day
They should awake, and find you gone.

II.

Live on, love on! Let reason swerve;
But instinct knows her own great lore,
Like some uncharted planet's curve
That sweeps in sight, then is no more.

Live on, love on, without a qualm,
Child of immortal charity,
In the great certitude and calm

Of joy free-born that shall not die.

III.

We dream ourselves inheritors
Of some unknown and distant good,
That shall requite us for the faults
Of our own lax ineptitude.

But soon and surely they may come,
Whom love makes wise and courage free,
Into their heritage of joy,
Their earth-day of eternity.

IV.

The thought that I could ever call
Your name, and you would not be here,
At moments sweeps my soul away
In the relentless tide of fear;

Then from its awful ebb returns
The sea of gladness strong and sure.
By this I know that love is great;
By this I know I shall endure.

V.

When I shall have lain down to sleep,
I pray no sound to break my rest.
No seraph's trumpet through the night
Could touch my weary soul with zest.

But oh, beyond the reach of thought
How I should waken and rejoice,
To hear across the drift of time
One golden echo of your voice!

AT THE GREAT RELEASE

When the black horses from the house of Dis
Stop at my door and the dread charioteer
Knocks at my portal, summoning me to go

On the far solitary unknown way
Where all the race of men fare and are lost,
Fleeting and numerous as the autumnal leaves
Before the wind in Lesbos of the Isles;

Though a chill draught of fear may quell my soul
And dim my spirit like a flickering lamp
In the great gusty hall of some old king,
Only one mordant unassuaged regret,
One passionate eternal human grief,
Would wring my heart with bitterness and tears
And set the mask of sorrow on my face.

Not youth, nor early fame, nor pleasant days,
Nor flutes, nor roses, nor the taste of wine,
Nor sweet companions of the idle hour
Who brought me tender joys, nor the glad sound
Of children's voices playing in the dusk;
All these I could forget and bid good-bye
And pass to my oblivion nor repine.

Not the green woods that I so dearly love,
Nor summer hills in their serenity,
Nor the great sea mystic and musical,
Nor drone of insects, nor the call of birds,
Nor soft spring flowers, nor the wintry stars;
To all the lovely earth that was my home
Smiling and valiant I could say farewell.

But not, oh, not to one strong little hand,
To one droll mouth brimming with witty words,
Nor ever to the unevasive eyes
Where dwell the light and sweetness of the world
With all the sapphire sparkle of the sea!
Ah, Destiny, against whose knees we kneel
With prayer at evening, spare me this one woe!

MORNING AND EVENING

When the morning wind comes up the mountain,
Stirring all the beech-groves of the valley,
And, before the paling stars have vanished,
The first tawny thrush disturbs the twilight
With his reed-pipe, eerie calm and golden —
The earth-music marvellous and olden —

Then good fortune enters at my doorway,
And my heart receives the guest called Gladness;
For I know it is that day of summer
When I shall behold your face ere nightfall,
And this earth, as never yet in story,
Ledge to hill-crest dyed in purple glory.

When the evening breath draws down the valley,
And the clove is full of dark blue shadows
Moving on the mountain- wall, just silvered
By the large moon lifted o'er the earth-rim,
At the moment of transported being,
When soul gathers what the eyes are seeing,

Sense is parted like a melted rain-mist,
And our mortal spirits run together,
Saying, "O incomparable comrade!"
Saying, "O my lover, how good love is!"
Then the twilight falls; the hill-wind hushes;
Note by note once more the cool-voiced thrushes.

IN AN IRIS MEADOW

Once I found you in an iris meadow
Down between the seashore and the river,
Playing on a golden willow whistle
You had fashioned from a bough in springtime,
Piping such a wild melodious music,
Full of sunshine, sadness and sweet longing,
As the heart of earth must have invented,
When the wind first breathed above her bosom.
And above the sea-rim, silver-lighted,
Pure and glad and innocent and tender,
The first melting planets glowed in splendour.

There it was I loved you as a lover,
Then it was I lost the world forever.
For your slender fingers on the notches
Set free more than that mere earthly cadence,
Loosed the piercing stops of mortal passion,
Touched your wood-mate with the spell of wonder,
And the godhead in the man awakened.
Virgin spirit with unsullied senses,
There was earth for him all new-created,
In a moment when the music's rapture
Bade soul take what never thought could capture:

Just the sheer glad bliss of being human,
Just the large content beyond all reason,
Just the love of flowers, hills and rivers,
Shadowy forests and lone lovely bird-songs
When the morning brightens in the sea-wind;
And beyond all these the fleeting vision
Of the shining soul that dwelt within you,
(Magic fragrance of the meadow blossom)
All the dear fond madness of the lover.
These, all these the ancient wood-god taught me
From the theme you piped and the wind brought me.

Was it strange that I should stop the playing?
Was it strange that I should touch the blossom?
Must (a man's way!) see whence came the music,
Must with childish marvel count the petals?
O but sweet were your uncounted kisses!
Wild and dear those first impulsive fondlings,
When your great eyes swept me, then went seaward,
Too o'ercharged to bear the strain of yearning,
And the little head must seek this shoulder!
Then we heard once more the wood-god's measure,
And strange gladness filled the world's great leisure.

A LETTER FROM LESBOS

More beloved than ever yet was mortal!
Oh, but doubt not, lover, I do love thee!
When he wrote these words, bitter and lonely
Was that tender heart in wintry Lesbos.
Kindly gods but speed my journey thither,
(How the wind burns from the scorching desert,
Through the scarlet beds of scentless blossom!)
And make fortunate that swift home-coming!
For I fret in this Egyptian exile,
Too long parted, sickening for the home-wind
And the first white gleam of Mitylene.

Blessed words to brave the stormy sea-way!
In this stifling city's sultry languor
I must now with joy and tears and longing,
Now the hundredth time at least re-read them:

It is the bitter season of the year;
The mournful-piping sea-wind is abroad

With driving snow and battle in the air,
Shaking the stubborn roof tree gust by gust;
And under the frost-grey skies without a sun
Cold desolation wraps the wintry world.

And I, my Gorgo, keep the fireside here,
Chill-hearted, brooding, visited by doubt,
Wondering how Demeter or wise Pan
Will work the resurrection of the spring,
Serene and punctual at the appointed time,
With the warm sun, the swallows at the eaves,
The slant of rain upon the purple hill,
The flame-like crocus by the garden wall,
The light, the hope, the gladness all returned
With maidens singing the Adonis song!

But ah, more doubtful sad and full of fear
There comes to me, disconsolate and lone,
The thought of thee, my Gorgo, lovelier
Than any premonition of the spring.

I seem to see that radiant smile once more,
The heaven-blue eyes, the crocus-golden hair,
The rose-pink beauty passionate and tall,
Dear beyond words and daring with desire,
For which thy lover would fling life away
And traffic the last legacy of time.

Ah, Gorgo, too long absent, well I know
The sun will shine again and spring come back
Her ancient glorious golden-flowered way,
And gladness visit the green earth once more,
But where in all that wonder wilt thou be,
The very soul and spirit of the spring?

If the high gods in that triumphant time
Have calendared no day for thee to come
Light-hearted to this doorway as of old,
Unmoved I shall behold their pomps go by,
The painted seasons in their pageantry,
The silvery processions of the moon,
And all the infinite ardours unsubdued,
Pass with the wind replenishing the earth.

Incredulous forever I must live,
And, once thy lover, without joy behold
The gradual uncounted years go by,
Sharing the bitterness of all things made.

Ah, not thus! My hot tears sweet and tender,
And the storm within this heaving bosom,
Could he see, would tell him what the truth is, —
How the heart of Gorgo breaks to reach him,
And her arms are weak with empty waiting
Through this long monotony of summer.
Gentle spirit, grieve not so, for love's sake!
How he raves beyond the touch of reason:

O heart of mine, be hardier for ills,
Since thou hast shared the sorrows of the gods
And been partaker of their destiny.
Have I not known the bitterness that sighed
In mournful grief upon the river marge,
And once obscured the lonely shining sun,
When Syrinx and when Daphne fled away?
Not otherwise in sorrow did I fare
Whom Gorgo, loveliest of mortals, loved,
And whose own folly that same Gorgo lost.

O lovers, hear me! Be not lax in love,
Nor let the loved one from you for a day.
For time that is the enemy of love,
And change that is the constant foe of man,
But wait the turn of opportunity
To fret the delicate fabric of our life
With doubt and slow forgetfulness and grief,
Till he who was a lover once goes forth
A friendless soul to front the joyless years,
A brooding uncompanioned wanderer
Beneath the silent and majestic stars.

Now what folly waits on brooding passion!
Truly not in solitude do mortals
Reach the height and nobleness of heroes.
Can it be so swiftly fades remembrance?
Oh, my fond heart prompt him! This is better:

The red flower of the fire is on the hearth,
The white flower of the foam is on the sea.
The golden marshes and the tawny dunes
Are gleaming white with snow and flushed with rose
Where the pure level wintry sunlight falls.
In the rose-garden, crimsoning each bough
Against the purple boulders in the wall,
Shine the rose-berries careless of the cold.
While down along the margin of the sea,

Just where the grey beach melts to greener grey,
With mounting wavering combing plunge and charge,
The towering breakers crumble in to shore.

Now from that quiet picture of the eye,
Hark to the trampling thunder and long boom,
The lone unscansioned and mysterious rote
Whose cadence marked the building of the world s
The old reverberant music of the sea!

Ah, to what ghostly piping of strange flutes
Strays in lost loveliness Persephone,
Heavy at heart, with trouble in her eyes,
From her deep-bosomed mother far away,
In the pale garden of Aidoneus now?
And oh, what delicate piping holds thee, too,
My Kore of the beauteous golden head?

What voice, what luring laughter bid thee stay
So long from thine own lover and so far?
Who touches with soft words thy tender heart,
In some bright foreign city far from here,
My unforgotten Gorgo beautiful?

Doubting still? O bitterest of absence
That the moth of doubt should mar the texture
And fine tissue of the spirit's garment,
The one garb of beauty which the soul wears, —
Love, the frailest, costliest of fabrics!
Ah, doubt not! O lover, lover, lover,
Who first taught the childlike heart of mortals
This most false and evil worldly wisdom?
Blighting as a frost on budded aloes,
How it blackens love, the golden blossom!
Would that I could cherish him this instant,
And dissolve that aching wintry passion
In the warmth of this impatient bosom!
By what cruel fate must I be banished
From his lonely bed? In lovely Lesbos
All my heart is, with its passionate longing.
O too piteous is the lot of women:

In the long night I lie awake for hours
Or sleep the sleep of dreamers without rest.
For in my soul there is discouragement,
And cold remorse lays hands upon my heart.
Now thou art gone, the grey world has no joy,
But bleak and bitter is the wind of life,

Cutting this timid traveller to the bone.

Not all the gods can ever give me peace,
Nor their forgiveness make me glad again,
For I have sinned against my own great soul
And cherished far too little thy great love.
Brave was thy spirit, glad and beautiful,
Nor ever faltered nor was faint of heart
In the fair splendid path of thy desire.
Even as I speak there comes a touch of shame,
Like a friend's hand upon my shoulder laid,
To think such moody and unmanly words
Could ever pass the mouth thy mouth has pressed.

Remembrance wakes. I hear the long far call
To fortitude and courage in the night
From my companions of the mighty past,
All the heroic lovers of the world.

Hast thou not had a sudden thought of me,
Unanxious, gay and tender with desire,
O thou beloved more than all mortal things?
For in my heart there was a sudden sense
Just now with presage of returning joy,
As when the wood-flowers waken to the sun
And all their lovely ardours re-arise,
Or when the sinking tide from utmost ebb
With one long sob summons his might once more.

Out of this winter will put forth one day
The incommunicable germ of spring,
The magic fervour that makes all things new,
When all the golden season will be glad
With soft south winds and birds and woodland flowers
And the shrill marshy music of the frogs,
Piping a chorus to their father Pan.
Then thou and I shall walk the earth once more
Delirious with each other as of old,
And the soft madness lead us far away
By meadowy roads and through the lilac hills
To our own province in the lands of love, —
My new-found Gorgo, heart-throb of the spring.

Heart of me! Ah, Cyprian deal gently!
Soon, Oh soon, restore me to my lover,
That I may repair this outworn habit,
And re-clothe him with thy golden glory,
Scarlet circumstance and purple splendour, —

State and air and pride of the immortals,
Which these mortal men, by our devising
And thy favour, wear — with fleeting rapture!
Fiercer blow, thou fervour of the desert!
Northward, northward, you hot winds of Nilus,
More consuming than a smelter's furnace!
You who do the will of alien Isis,
To this heart you cannot be unfriendly,
If I once may loose the sail for Lesbos,
And along the green and foaming sea-track
Scud before you, light as any swallow
Flashing down the long blue slope of springtime.
O ye home-gods, free me to my lover!

THE PLAYERS

We are the players of a play
As old as earth,
Between the wings of night and day,
With tears and mirth.

There is no record of the land
From whence it came,
No legend of the playwright's hand,
No bruited fame

Of those who for the piece were cast
On that first night,
When God drew up His curtain vast
And there was light.

Before our eyes as we come on,
From age to age,
Flare up the footlights of the dawn
On this round stage.

In front, unknown, beyond the glare
Vague shadows loom;
And sounds like muttering winds are there
Foreboding doom.

Yet wistfully we keep the boards;
And as we mend
The blundering forgotten words,
Hope to the end

To hear the storm-beat of applause
Fill our desire
When the dark Prompter gives us pause,
And we retire.

THE MANSION

I thought it chill and lonesome,
And too far from the road
For an ideal dwelling,
When here I first abode.

But yesterday a lodger
Smiled as she passed my door,
With mien of gay contentment
That lured me to explore.

Unerringly she leads me,
Compassionate and wise,
Soul of immortal beauty
Wearing the mortal guise.

She knows from sill to attic
The great house through and through,
Its treasures of the ages,
Surprises ever new.

From room to room I follow,
Entranced with each in turn,
Enchanted by each wonder
She bids my look discern.

She names them: here is First-love,
A chamber by the sea;
Here in a flood of noonday
Is spacious Charity.

Here is a cell, Devotion;
And lonely Courage here,
Where child-deserted windows
Look on the Northern year;

Friendship and Faith and Gladness,
Fragrant of air and bloom,
Where one might spend a lifetime
Secure from fear of gloom.

And often as we wander,
I fancy we have neared
The Master of the Mansion,
Who has not yet appeared.

WHO IS THE OWNER?

Who owns this house, my lord or I?
He in whose name the title runs,
Or I, who keep it swept and clean
And open to the winds and suns?

He who is absent year by year,
On some far pleasure of his own,
Or I who spend on it so much
Of willing flesh and aching bone?

What if it prove a fable, all
This rumour of a legal lord,
And we should find ourselves in truth
Owners and masters of the board!

What if this earth should just belong
To those who tend it, you and me!
What if for once we should refuse
His rental to this absentee?

O friends, no landlord in the world
Could love the place as well as I!
Love is the owner of the house,
The only lord of destiny.

THE FAIRY FLOWER

There's a fairy flower that grows
In a corner of my heart,
And the fragrance that it spills
Is the sorcery of art.

I may give it little care,
Neither water it nor prune,
Yet it suddenly will blow
Glorious beneath the moon.

I may tend it night and day,
Taking thought to make it bloom;
Yet my efforts all will fail
To avert the touch of doom.

When it dies, my little flower,
You may take my life as well;
Though I live a hundred years,
I shall have no more to tell.

YVANHOÉ FERRARA

Teach me, of little worth, O Fame,
The golden word that shall proclaim
Yvanhoé Ferrara's name.

I would that I might rest me now,
As once I rested long ago,

In the dim purple summer night,
On scented linen cool and white,

Lulled by the murmur of the sea
And thy soft breath, Yvanhoé.

What cared we for the world or time,
Though like a far-off fitful chime,

We heard the mournful anchored bell
Above the sunken reef foretell

That time should pass and pleasure be
No more for us, Yvanhoé!

We saw the crimson sun go down
Across the harbour and the town,

Dyeing the roofs and spars with gold;
But all his magic, ages old,

Was not so wonderful to me
As thy gold hair, Yvanhoé.

Between the window and the road
The tall red poppies burned and glowed;

They moved and flickered like a flame,
As the low sea-wind went and came;

But redder and more warm than they,
Was thy red mouth, Yvanhoé.

I think the stars above the hill
Upon the brink of time stood still;

And the great breath of life that blows
The coal-bright sun, the flame-bright rose,

Entered the room and kindled thee
As in a forge, Yvanhoé

Prospered the ruddy fire, and fanned
Thy beauty to a rosy brand,

Till all the odorous purple dark
Reeled, and thy soul became a spark

In the great draught of Destiny
Which men call love, Yvanhoé.

The untold ardour of the earth
That knows no sorrow, fear nor dearth,

Before the pent-up moment passed,
Was glad of all its will at last

And more, if such a thing could be
In thy long kiss, Yvanhoé.

For years my life was bright and glad,
Because of the great joy we had;

Until I heard the wind repeat
Thy name behind me in the street,

Like a lost lyric of the sea,
" Yvanhoé, Yvanhoé."

But now the day has no desire;
The scarlet poppies have no fire;

There is no magic in the sun
Nor anything he shines upon;

Only the muttering of the sea,
Since thou art dead, Yvanhoé.

Now God on high, be mine the blame,
If time destroy or men defame
Yvanhoé Ferrara's name.

THE LOVE-CHANT OF KING HACKO

In the time of red October,
In the hills of the pointed fir,
In the days of the slanted sunlight
That ripens cone and burr,
God gave me a splendid woman —
A mate for a lord of lands —
And put the madness on me,
And left her there in my hands.

In the roving woodland season,
When the afternoons are still
And the sound of lowing cattle
Comes up to the purple hill,
God would speak to His creatures,
Flower and beast and bird,
And lays the silence upon them
To hearken to His word.

In the time of the scarlet maple,
When the blue Indian haze
Walks through the wooded valley
And sleeps by the mountain ways,
She stood like a beech in the forest,
Where the wash of sunlight lies,
With her wonderful beech-red hair
And her wondering beech-grey eyes.

In the time of the apple harvest,
When the fruit is gold on the bough,
She stood in the moted sunshine,
The orchards remember how
Loving, untrammelled and generous,
Ardent and supple and tall,
Quick to the breath of the spirit
As a shadow that moves on a wall.

In a yellow and crimson valley,
At the time of the turning leaf,
When warm are the tawny fern-beds,
And the cricket's life is brief,
I saw the dark blood mantle
And prosper under the tan,
Then I knew the power God lent me
To use, when He made me man.

The world, all being and beauty
From meadow to mountain-line,
Awaiting the touch of rapture
For a meaning and a sign;
A woman's voice said, "Hacko,"
Then I knew and could understand
How love is a greater province
Than dominion of sea or land.

In the month of golden hillsides,
When moons are frosty white,
And the returning Hunter
Looms on the marge of night,
Relieving his brother Arcturus,
Belted, majestic and slow,
To patrol the Arctic watch-fires
And sentry the lands of snow,

A core of fire was kindled
On a hearthstone wide and deep,
Where the great arms of the mountains
Put Folly-of-mind to sleep;
We came without guide or knowledge,
Silver, array or store,
Through the land of purple twilight
To the lodge of the Open Door.

THE CREATION OF LILITH

This happened in the Garden
Ages on ages since,
When noontide made a pleasant shade
Of ilex, pear and quince.

The Gardener sat and pondered
Some beauty rarer still
Than any he had wrought of earth

And fashioned to his will.

"Now who will be her body?"
"I," said the splendid rose,
"Colour, fire and fragrance,
In imperial repose."

"Who will be her two eyes?"
"I," said the flag of blue,
"Sky and sea all shadowy
Drench me wholly through."

"Who will be her bright mouth?"
"I," the carnation said,
"With my old Eastern ardour
And my Persian red."

"Who will be, among you,
The glory of her hair?"
His glance went reaching through the noon;
The marigold was there.

"Who will be her laughter,
Her love-word and her sigh?"
Among the whispering tree-tops
A breath of wind said, "I."

"And whence will come her spirit?"
Answer there was none.
The Gardener breathed upon her mouth,
And lo, there had been done

The miracle of beauty
Outmarvelling the flowers;
While the great blue dial
Recorded the slow hours.

IN A FAR COUNTRY

In a land that is little traversed,
Beyond the news of the town,
There lies a delectable Kingdom
Where the crimson sun goes down,

The province of fruitlands and flowers
And colour and sea-sounds and love.

If you were queen of that country,
And I were the king thereof,

We should tread upon scarlet poppies,
And be glad the long day through,
Where the bluest skies in the world
Rest upon hills of blue.

We should wander the slopes of the mountains
With the wind and the nomad bee,
And watch the white sails on the sea-rim
Come up from the curving sea.

We should watch from the sides of the valleys
The caravans of the rain,
In trappings of purple and silver,
Go by on the far-off plain.

And they all should be freighted with treasure,
The vision that gladdens the eye,
The beauty that betters the spirit
To sustain it by and by.

We should hear the larks' fine field-notes
Breaking in bubbly swells,
As if from their rocking steeples
The lilies were ringing their bells;

We should hear invisible fingers
Play on the strings of the pines
The broken measure whose motive
Only a lover divines;

The music of Earth, the enchantress,
The cadence that dwells in the heart
Against the time of oblivion,
To bid it remember and start.

And nothing should make us unhappy,
And no one should make us afraid,
For we should be royal lovers
In the land where this plot is laid.

And with night on the almond orchards
We should lie w y here warm winds creep,
Under the starry tent-cloth
Hearing the footfall of Sleep.

SONG O F THE FOUR WORLDS

I.

Is it northward, little friend?
And she whispered, "What is there?"

There are people who are loyal to the glory of their past,
Who held by heart's tradition, and will hold it to the last;
Who would not sell in shame
The honour of their name,
Though the world were in the balance and a sword thereon were cast.

Oh, there the ice is breaking, the brooks are running free,
A robin calls at twilight from a tall spruce-tree,
And the light canoes go down
Past portage, camp and town,
By the rivers that make murmur in the lands along the sea.

And she said, "It is not there,
Though I love you, love you dear;
I cannot bind my little heart with loves of yester year."

II.

Is it southward, little friend?
"Lover, what is there? "

There are men of many nations who were sick of strife and gain,
And only ask forgetfulness of all the old world's pain.
There Life sets down her measure
For Time to fill at leisure
With loveliness and plenty in the islands of the main.

Oh, there the palms are rustling, the oranges are bright;
In all the little harbour towns the coral streets are white;
The scarlet flowers fall
By the creamy convent wall,
And the Southern Cross gets up from sea to steer the purple night.

And she said, "It is not there,
Though I love you, love you dear;
I should weary of the beauty that is changeless all the year."

III.

Is it eastward, little friend
And she whispered, "What is there?"

There are rivers good for healing, there are temples in the hills,
There men forsake desire and put by their earthly wills;
And there the old earth breeds
Her mystic mighty creeds
For the lifting of all burdens and the loosing of all ills.

Oh, the tents are in the valley where the shadows sleep at noon,
Where the pack-train halts at twilight and the spicy bales are strewn,
Where the long brown road goes by
To the cut against the sky,
And is lost within the circle of the silent, rosy moon.

And she said, "It is not there,
Though I love you, love you dear;
For my faith is warm and living, not unearthly,
old and sere."

IV.

Is it westward, little friend?
"Lover, what is there?"

There are men and women who are sovereigns of their fate,
Who look Despair between the eyes and know that they are great;
Who will not halt nor quail
On the eager endless trail,
Till Destiny makes way for them and Love unbars the gate.

Oh, there the purple lilies are blowing in the sun,
And the meadow larks are singing a thousand, if there's one!
And the long blue hills arise
To the wondrous dreamy skies,
For the twisted azure columns of the rain to rest upon.

And she said, "It is not there,
For I love you, love you dear.
Oh, shut the door on Sorrow, for the Four
Great Worlds are here!"

STREET SONG AT NIGHT

There's many a quiet seaport that waits the daring sail;
There's many a lonely farer by many a doubtful trail.
And what should be their star
To lead them safe and far, —
What guide to take them o'er the crest, what pilot past the bar,
Save Love, the great adventurer who will not turn nor quail?

As a voyager might remember how the face of earth was changed, —
All the dreary grey of winter forgotten and estranged, —
When he rode the tempest through
And steered into the blue
Of a tranquil tropic morning diaphanous and new,
With palms upon the sea-rim where the flying-fishes ranged;

As a lover in old story on a night of wind and rain
Might have stood beneath a window, till a lamp should light the pane
And a lady lean one arm
On the glowing square and warm, —
A girlish golden figure in a frame of dark and storm, —
To look the longest moment ere he turned to life again,

Then set a stubborn shoulder to wind and sleet and snow,
With the weather foul above him and the pavement foul below;
So it happened in my case;
When I saw her, every trace
Of doubt and fear and languor to the pulse of joy gave place,
And the world was great and goodly as he planned it long ago.

There's a shipman who goes sailing where the sea is round and high;
There's a lover who goes piping where winds of morning cry;
And the lilt beneath his heart
Was timed to stop and start,
Till no more ships go sailing and the green hills fall apart.
O, friends, that minstrel-lover, that mariner am I.

THE LEAST OF LOVE

Only let one fair frail woman
Mourn for me when I am dead,
World, withhold your best of praises!
There are better things instead.

Shall the little fame concern me,
Or the triumph of the years,
When I keep the mighty silence,

Through the falling of her tears?

I shall heed not, though 'twere April
And my field-larks all returned,
When her lips upon these eyelids
One last poppied kiss have burned.

Painted hills shall not allure me,
Mirrored in the painted stream;
Having loved them, I shall leave them,
Busy with the vaster dream.

Only let one dear dark woman
Mourn for me when I am dead,
I shall be content with beauty
And the dust above my head.

Yet when I shall make the journey
From these earthly dear abodes,
I have four things to remember
At the Crossing of the Roads.

How her hand was like a tea-rose;
And her low voice like the South;
Her soft eyes were tarns of sable;
A red poppy was her mouth.

Only let one sweet frail woman
Mourn for me when I am dead,
Gently for her gentlest lover,
More than all will have been said.

Be my requiem the rain-wind;
And my immortality
But the lifetime of one heartache
By the unremembering sea!

A MAN'S LAST WORD

Death said to me,
"Three things I ask of thee;
And thy reply
Shall make thee or undo thee presently."

I said, "Say on,
Lord Death, thy will be done.

One answers now,
To bribe and fear indifferent as thou."

He said, "Behold,
My power is from of old.
The drunken sea
Is but a henchman and a serf to me.

"Hunger and war
My tireless sleuth-hounds are.
Before my nod
The quailing nations have no help but God.

"What hast thou found,
In one life's little round,
Stronger than these?"
I said, "One little hand-touch of Marie's."

He said, "Again:
Of all brave sights to men —
The glittering rain,
A towering city in an autumn plain,

"An eagle's flight,
A beacon-fire at night,
The harvest moon,
The burnish of a marching host at noon —

"What hast thou seen
In one life's small demesne,
Fairer than these?"
I said, "That supple body of Marie's."

He said, "Once more:
Of all men labour for,
Battle and yearn,
And spend their blessed days without return

"Leisure or wealth,
Or power or sun-tanned health,
A bruited name,
Or the sad solace of a little fame

"What hast thou known,
In one life's narrow zone,
Dearer than these?"
I said, "One little love-kiss of Marie's."

And then Death said,
"To-day among the dead
Thou shalt go down,
And with the wise receive thy just renown."

A MIDWINTER MEMORY

Now the snow is on the roof,
Now the wind is in the flue,
Beauty, keep no more aloof,
Make my winter dreaming true,
Give my fancy proof.

How the year runs back to June,
To the day I saw you first!
In the sultry afternoon
There the mountains lay immersed
In a summer swoon.

In the orchard with your book,
I can see you now as then
That serene and smiling look,
Far away and back again,
While my spirit shook.

Now the frost is on the pane,
And the winter on the sea,
Gold across the iron strain,
Thought of you comes back to me,
Like a lost refrain.

What a voice it was I heard!
All your j's were soft as d's,
Like the nest-notes of a bird,
And your fingers clasped your knees,
As you smiled each word.

Well I knew you for the one
Sought so long and never found,
In this country of the sun,
All these burning summers round.
There, the search was done!

Now the dark is at the door;
Now the snow is on the sill;
And for all I may deplore,

Time must have his ancient will
Mar one lover more.

AN ANGEL IN PLASTER

Dear smiling little snub-nosed baby face
With angel wings,
Be them the guardian of this house, and grace
Its sublunary things.

Look laughing down, O blessed babe, and lend
That guileless charm,
That beaming joy, to sweeten and defend
Our dwelling from all harm.

Bid sorrow shun the threshold of this door,
And memory
Cease in this place forever to deplore
What has been and must be.

Come sun or storm, come merriment or tears,
No care can fret
Thy radiant spirit, nor the heavy years
Invade it with regret.

Surely thou art a traveller from a land
That knows no grief!
The life of men thou canst not understand
So turbulent, so brief.

Yet thou must tarry here, thou darling one,
To smile and bring
Thoughts of the world's fair youth, a fadeless sun
And a perpetual spring.

Bliss Carman - An Appreciation

How many Canadians—how many even among the few who seek to keep themselves informed of the best in contemporary literature, who are ever on the alert for the new voices—realise, or even suspect, that this Northern land of theirs has produced a poet of whom it may be affirmed with confidence and assurance that he is of the great succession of English poets? Yet such—strange and unbelievable though it may seem—is in very truth the case, that poet being (to give him his full name) William Bliss Carman. Canada has full right to be proud of her poets, a small body though they are; but not only does Mr. Carman stand high and clear above them all—his place (and time cannot but confirm and justify the assertion) is among those men whose poetry is the shining glory of that great English literature which is our common heritage.

If any should ask why, if what has been just said is so, there has been—as must be admitted—no general recognition of the fact in the poet's home land, I would answer that there are various and plausible, if not good, reasons for it.

First of all, the poet, as thousands more of our young men of ambition and confidence have done, went early to the United States, and until recently, except for rare and brief visits to his old home down by the sea, has never returned to Canada—though for all that, I am able to state, on his own authority, he is still a Canadian citizen. Then all his books have had their original publication in the United States, and while a few of them have subsequently carried the imprints of Canadian publishers, none of these can be said ever to have made any special effort to push their sale. Another reason for the fact above mentioned is that Mr. Carman has always scorned to advertise himself, while his work has never been the subject of the log-rolling and booming which the work of many another poet has had—to his ultimate loss. A further reason is that he follows a rule of his own in preparing his books for publication. Most poets publish a volume of their work as soon as, through their industry and perseverance, they have material enough on hand to make publication desirable in their eyes. Not so with Mr. Carman, however, his rule being not to publish until he has done sufficient work of a certain general character or key to make a volume. As a result, you cannot fully know or estimate his work by one book, or two books, or even half a dozen; you must possess or be familiar with every one of the score and more volumes which contain his output of poetry before you can realise how great and how many-sided is his genius.

It is a common remark on the part of those who respond readily to the vigorous work of Kipling, or Masefield, even our own Service, that Bliss Carman's poetry has no relation to or concern with ordinary, everyday life. One would suppose that most persons who cared for poetry at all turned to it as a relief from or counter to the burdens and vexations of the daily round; but in any event, the remark referred to seems to me to indicate either the most casual acquaintance with Mr. Carman's work, or a complete misunderstanding and misapprehension of the meaning of it. I grant that you will find little or nothing in it all to remind you of the grim realities and vexing social problems of this modern existence of ours; but to say or to suggest that these things do not exist for Mr. Carman is to say or to suggest something which is the reverse of true. The truth is, he is aware of them as only one with the sensitive organism of a poet can be; but he does not feel that he has a call or mission to remedy them, and still less to sing of them. He therefore leaves the immediate problems of the day to those who choose, or are led, to occupy themselves therewith, and turns resolutely away to dwell upon those things which for him possess infinitely greater importance.

"What are they?" one who knows Mr. Carman only as, say, a lyrist of spring or as a singer of the delights of vagabondia probably will ask in some wonder. Well, the things which concern him above all, I would answer, are first, and naturally, the beauty and wonder of this world of ours, and next the mystery of the earthly pilgrimage of the human soul out of eternity and back into it again.

The poems in the present volume—which, by the way, can boast the high honor of being the very first regular Canadian edition of his work—will be evidence ample and conclusive to every reader, I am sure, of the place which

The perennial enchanted

Lovely world and all its lore

occupy in the heart and soul of Bliss Carman, as well as of the magical power with which he is able to convey the deep and unfailing satisfaction and delight which they possess for him. They, however, represent his latest period (he has had three well-defined periods), comprising selections from three of his last published volumes: The Rough Rider, Echoes from Vagabondia, and April Airs, together with a number of new poems, and do not show, except here and there and by hints and flashes, how great is his preoccupation with the problem of man's existence—

—the hidden import
Of man's eternal plight.

This is manifest most in certain of his earlier books, for in these he turns and returns to the greatest of all the problems of man almost constantly, probing, with consummate and almost unrivalled use of the art of expression, for the secret which surely, he clearly feels, lies hidden somewhere, to be discovered if one could but pierce deeply enough. Pick up Behind the Arras, and as you turn over page after page you cannot but observe how incessantly the poet's mind—like the minds of his two great masters, Browning and Whitman—works at this problem. In "Behind the Arras," the title poem; "In the Wings," "The Crimson House," "The Lodger," "Beyond the Gamut," "The Juggler"—yes, in every poem in the book—he takes up and handles the strange thing we know as, or call, life, turning it now this way, now that, in an effort to find out its meaning and purpose. He comes but little nearer success in this than do most of the rest of men, of course; but the magical and ever-fresh beauty of his expression, the haunting melody of his lines, the variety of his images and figures and the depth and range of his thought, put his searchings and ponderings in a class by themselves.

Lengthy quotation from Mr. Carman's books is not permitted here, and I must guide myself accordingly, though with reluctance, because I believe that in a study such as this the subject should be allowed to speak for himself as much as possible. In "Behind the Arras" the poet describes the passage from life to death as

A cadence dying down unto its source
In music's course,

and goes on to speak of death as

—the broken rhythm of thought and man,
The sweep and span
Of memory and hope
About the orbit where they still must grope
For wider scope,

To be through thousand springs restored, renewed,
With love imbrued,
With increments of will
Made strong, perceiving unattainment still
From each new skill.

Now follow some verses from "Behind the Gamut," to my mind the poet's greatest single achievement;

As fine sand spread on a disc of silver,
At some chord which bids the motes combine,
Heeding the hidden and reverberant impulse,
Shifts and dances into curve and line,

The round earth, too, haply, like a dust-mote,
Was set whirling her assigned sure way,
Round this little orb of her ecliptic
To some harmony she must obey.

And what of man?

Linked to all his half-accomplished fellows,
Through unfrontiered provinces to range—
Man is but the morning dream of nature,
Roused to some wild cadence weird and strange.

Here, now, are some verses from "Pulvis et Umbra," which is to be found in Mr. Carman's first book, Low
Tide on Grand Pré, and in which the poet addresses a moth which a storm has blown into his window:

For man walks the world with mourning
Down to death and leaves no trace,
With the dust upon his forehead,
And the shadow on his face.

Pillared dust and fleeing shadow
As the roadside wind goes by,
And the fourscore years that vanish
In the twinkling of an eye.

"Pillared dust and fleeing shadow." Where in all our English literature will one find the life history of
man summed up more briefly and, at the same time, more beautifully, than in that wonderful line? Now
follows a companion verse to those just quoted, taken from "Lord of My Heart's Elation," which stands
in the forefront of From the Green Book of the Bards. It may be remarked here that while the poet
recurs again and again to some favorite thought or idea, it is never in the same words. His expression is
always new and fresh, showing how deep and true is his inspiration. Again it is man who is pictured:

A fleet and shadowy column
Of dust and mountain rain,
To walk the earth a moment
And be dissolved again.

But while Mr. Carman's speculations upon life's meaning and the mystery of the future cannot but
appeal to the thoughtful-minded, it is as an interpreter of nature that he makes his widest appeal. Bliss
Carman, I must say here, and emphatically, is no mere landscape-painter; he never, or scarcely ever,
paints a picture of nature for its own sake. He goes beyond the outward aspect of things and interprets
or translates for us with less keen senses as only a poet whose feeling for nature is of the deepest and

profoundest, who has gone to her whole-heartedly and been taken close to her warm bosom, can do. Is this not evident from these verses from "The Great Return"—originally called "The Pagan's Prayer," and for some inscrutable reason to be found only in the limited Collected Poems, issued in two stately volumes in 1905.

When I have lifted up my heart to thee,
Thou hast ever hearkened and drawn near,
And bowed thy shining face close over me,
Till I could hear thee as the hill-flowers hear.

When I have cried to thee in lonely need,
Being but a child of thine bereft and wrung,
Then all the rivers in the hills gave heed;
And the great hill-winds in thy holy tongue—

That ancient incommunicable speech—
The April stars and autumn sunsets know—
Soothed me and calmed with solace beyond reach
Of human ken, mysterious and low.

Who can read or listen to those moving lines without feeling that Mr. Carman is in very truth a poet of nature—nay, Nature's own poet? But how could he be other when, in "The Breath of the Reed" (From the Green Book of the Bards), he makes the appeal?

Make me thy priest, O Mother,
And prophet of thy mood,
With all the forest wonder
Enraptured and imbued.

As becomes such a poet, and particularly a poet whose birth-month is April, Mr. Carman sings much of the early spring. Again and again he takes up his woodland pipe, and lo! Pan himself and all his train troop joyously before us. Yet the singer's notes for all his singing never become wearied or strident; his airs are ever new and fresh; his latest songs are no less spontaneous and winning than were his first, written how many years ago, while at the same time they have gained in beauty and melody. What heart will not stir to the vibrant music of his immortal "Spring Song," which was originally published in the first Songs from Vagabondia, and the opening verses of which follow?

Make me over, mother April,
When the sap begins to stir!
When thy flowery hand delivers
All the mountain-prisoned rivers,
And thy great heart beats and quivers
To revive the days that were,
Make me over, mother April,
When the sap begins to stir!

Take my dust and all my dreaming,
Count my heart-beats one by one,

Send them where the winters perish;
Then some golden noon recherish
And restore them in the sun,
Flower and scent and dust and dreaming,
With their heart-beats every one!

That poem is sufficient in itself to prove that Bliss Carman has full right and title to be called Spring's own lyrist, though it may be remarked here that not all his spring poems are so unfeignedly joyous. Many of them indeed, have a touch, or more than a touch, of wistfulness, for the poet knows well that sorrow lurks under all joy, deep and well hidden though it may be.

Mr. Carman sings equally finely, though perhaps not so frequently, of summer and the other seasons; but as he has other claims upon our attention, I shall forbear to labor the fact, particularly as the following collection demonstrates it sufficiently. One of those other claims is as a writer of sea poetry. Few poets, it may be said, have pictured the majesty and the mystery, the beauty and the terror of the sea, better than he. His Ballads of Lost Haven is a veritable treasure-house for those whose spirits find kinship in wide expanses of moving waters. One of the best known poems in this volume is "The Gravedigger," which opens thus:

Oh, the shambling sea is a sexton old,
And well his work is done.
With an equal grave for lord and knave,
He buries them every one.

Then hoy and rip, with a rolling hip,
He makes for the nearest shore;
And God, who sent him a thousand ship,
Will send him a thousand more;
But some he'll save for a bleaching grave,
And shoulder them in to shore—
Shoulder them in, shoulder them in,
Shoulder them in to shore.

In "The City of the Sea" (Last Songs from Vagabondia) Mr. Carman speaks of the seabells sounding

The eternal cadence of sea sorrow
For Man's lot and immemorial wrong—
The lost strains that haunt the human dwelling
With the ghost of song.

Elsewhere he speaks of

The great sea, mystic and musical.

And here from another poem is a striking picture:

... the old sea
Seems to whimper and deplore

Mourning like a childless crone
With her sorrow left alone—
The eternal human cry
To the heedless passer-by.

I have said above that Mr. Carman has had three distinct periods, and intimated that the poems in the following collection are of his third period. The first period may be said to be represented by the Low Tide and Behind the Arras volumes, while the second is displayed in the three volumes of Songs from Vagabondia, which he published in association with his friend Richard Hovey. Bliss Carman was from the first too original and individual a poet to be directly influenced by anyone else; but there can be no doubt that his friendship with Hovey helped to turn him from over-preoccupation with mysteries which, for all their greatness, are not for man to solve, to an intenser realisation of the beauty and loveliness of the world about him and of the joys of human fellowship. The result is seen in such poems as "Spring Song," quoted in part above, and his perhaps equally well-known "The Joys of the Road," which appeared in the same volume with that poem, and a few verses from which follow:

Now the joys of the road are chiefly these:
A crimson touch on the hardwood trees;

A vagrant's morning wide and blue,
In early fall, when the wind walks, too;

A shadowy highway cool and brown,
Alluring up and enticing down

From rippled waters and dappled swamp,
From purple glory to scarlet pomp;

The outward eye, the quiet will,
And the striding heart from hill to hill.

Some of the finest of arman's work is contained in his elegiac or memorial poems, in which he commemorates Keats, Shelley, William Blake, Lincoln, Stevenson, and other men for whom he has a kindred feeling, and also friends whom he has loved and lost. Listen to these moving lines from "Non Omnis Moriar," written in memory of Gleeson White, and to be found in Last Songs from Vagabondia:

There is a part of me that knows,
Beneath incertitude and fear,
I shall not perish when I pass
Beyond mortality's frontier;

But greatly having joyed and grieved,
Greatly content, shall hear the sigh
Of the strange wind across the lone
Bright lands of taciturnity.

In patience therefore I await
My friend's unchanged benign regard,—

Some April when I too shall be
Spilt water from a broken shard.

In "The White Gull," written for the centenary of the birth of Shelley in 1892, and included in By the Aurelian Wall, he thus apostrophizes that clear and shining spirit:

O captain of the rebel host,
Lead forth and far!
Thy toiling troopers of the night
Press on the unavailing fight;
The sombre field is not yet lost,
With thee for star.

Thy lips have set the hail and haste
Of clarions free
To bugle down the wintry verge
Of time forever, where the surge
Thunders and trembles on a waste
And open sea.

In "A Seamark," a threnody for Robert Louis Stevenson, which appears in the same volume, the poet hails "R.L.S." (of whose tribe he may be said to be truly one) as

The master of the roving kind,

and goes on:

O all you hearts about the world
In whom the truant gypsy blood,
Under the frost of this pale time,
Sleeps like the daring sap and flood
That dreams of April and reprieve!
You whom the haunted vision drives,
Incredulous of home and ease.
Perfection's lovers all your lives!

You whom the wander-spirit loves
To lead by some forgotten clue
Forever vanishing beyond
Horizon brinks forever new;
Our restless loved adventurer,
On secret orders come to him,
Has slipped his cable, cleared the reef,
And melted on the white sea-rim.

"Perfection's lovers all your lives." Of these, it may be said without qualification, is Bliss Carman himself.

No summary of Mr. Carman's work, however cursory, would be worthy of the name if it omitted mention of his ventures in the realm of Greek myth. From the Book of Myths is made up of work of that sort, every poem in it being full of the beauty of phrase and melody of which Mr. Carman alone has the secret. The finest poems in the book, barring the opening one, "Overlord," are "Daphne," "The Dead Faun," "Hylas," and "At Phædra's Tomb," but I can do no more here than name them, for extracts would fail to reveal their full beauty. And beauty, after all is said, is the first and last thing with Mr. Carman. As he says himself somewhere:

The joy of the hand that hews for beauty
Is the dearest solace under the sun.

And again

The eternal slaves of beauty
Are the masters of the world.

A slave—a happy, willing slave—to beauty is the poet himself, and the world can never repay him for the message of beauty which he has brought it.

Kindred to From the Book of Myths, but much more important, is Sappho: One Hundred Lyrics, one of the most successful of the numerous attempts which have been made to recapture the poems by that high priestess of song which remain to us only in fragments. Mr. Carman, as Charles G. D. Roberts points out in an introduction to the volume, has made no attempt here at translation or paraphrasing; his venture has been "the most perilous and most alluring in the whole field of poetry"—that of imaginative and, at the same time, interpretive construction. Brief quotation again would fail to convey an adequate idea of the exquisiteness of the work, and all I can do, therefore, is to urge all lovers of real poetry to possess themselves of Sappho: One Hundred Lyrics, for it is literally a storehouse of lyric beauty.

I must not fail here to speak of From the Book of Valentines, which contains some lovely things, notably "At the Great Release." This is not only one of the finest of all Mr. Carman's poems, but it is also one of the finest poems of our time. It is a love poem, and no one possessing any real feeling for poetry can read it without experiencing that strange thrill of the spirit which only the highest form of poetry can communicate. "Morning and Evening," "In an Iris Meadow," and "A letter from Lesbos" must be also mentioned. In the last named poem, Sappho is represented as writing to Gorgo, and expresses herself in these moving words:

If the high gods in that triumphant time
Have calendared no day for thee to come
Light-hearted to this doorway as of old,
Unmoved I shall behold their pomps go by—
The painted seasons in their pageantry,
The silvery progressions of the moon,
And all their infinite ardors unsubdued,
Pass with the wind replenishing the earth

Incredulous forever I must live
And, once thy lover, without joy behold,

The gradual uncounted years go by,
Sharing the bitterness of all things made.

Mention must be now made of Songs of the Sea Children, which can be described only as a collection of the sweetest and tenderest love lyrics written in our time—

—the lyric songs
The earthborn children sing,
When wild-wood laughter throngs
The shy bird-throats of spring;
When there's not a joy of the heart
But flies like a flag unfurled,
And the swelling buds bring back
The April of the world.

So perfect and complete are these lyrics that it would be almost sacrilege to quote any of them unless entire. Listen however, to these verses:

The day is lost without thee,
The night has not a star.
Thy going is an empty room
Whose door is left ajar.

Depart: it is the footfall
Of twilight on the hills.
Return: and every rood of ground
Breaks into daffodils.

There are those who will have it that Bliss Carman has been away from Canada so long that he has ceased to be, in a real sense, a Canadian. Such assume rather than know, for a very little study of his work would show them that it is shot through and through with the poet's feeling for the land of his birth. Memories of his childhood and youthful years down by the sea are still fresh in Mr. Carman's mind, and inspire him again and again in his writing. "A Remembrance," at the beginning of the present collection, may be pointed to as a striking instance of this, but proof positive is the volume, Songs from a Northern Garden, for it could have been written only by a Canadian, born and bred, one whose heart and soul thrill to the thought of Canada. I would single out from this volume for special mention as being "Canadian" in the fullest sense "In a Grand Pré Garden," "The Keeper's Silence," "At Home and Abroad," "Killoleet," and "Above the Gaspereau," but have no space to quote from them.

But Mr. Carman is not only a Canadian, he is also a Briton; and evidence of this is his Ode on the Coronation, written on the occasion of the crowning of King Edward VII in 1902. This poem—the very existence of which is hardly known among us—ought to be put in the hands of every child and youth who speaks the English tongue, for no other, I dare maintain—nothing by Kipling, or Newbolt, or any other of our so-called "Imperial singers"—expresses more truly and more movingly the deep feeling of love and reverence which the very thought of England evokes in every son of hers, even though it may never have been his to see her white cliffs rise or to tread her storied ground:

O England, little mother by the sleepless Northern tide,

Having bred so many nations to devotion, trust, and pride,
Very tenderly we turn
With welling hearts that yearn
Still to love you and defend you,—let the sons of men discern
Wherein your right and title, might and majesty, reside.

In concluding this, I greatly fear, lamentably inadequate study, I come to the collection which follows, and which, as intimated above, represents the work of Mr. Carman's latest period. I must say at once that, while I yield to no one in admiration for Low Tide and the other books of that period, or for the work of the second period, as represented by the Songs from Vagabondia volumes, I have no hesitation in declaring that I regard the poet's work of the past few years with even higher admiration. It may not possess the force and vigor of the work which preceded it; but anything seemingly missing in that respect is more than made up for me by increased beauty and clarity of expression. The mysticism—verging, or more than verging, at times on symbolism—which marked his earlier poems, and which hung, as it were, as a veil between them and the reader, has gone, and the poet's thought or theme now lies clearly before us as in a mirror. What—to take a verse from the following pages at random—could be more pellucid, more crystal clear in expression—what indeed, could come closer to that achieving of the impossible at which every real poet must aim—than this from "In Gold Lacquer".

Gold are the great trees overhead,
And gold the leaf-strewn grass,
As though a cloth of gold were spread
To let a seraph pass.
And where the pageant should go by,
Meadow and wood and stream,
The world is all of lacquered gold,
Expectant as a dream.

The poet, happily, has fully recovered from the serious illness which laid him low some two years ago, and which for a time caused his friends and admirers the gravest concern, and so we may look forward hopefully to seeing further volumes of verse come from the press to make certain his name and fame. But if, for any reason, this should not be—which the gods forfend!—Later Poems, I dare affirm, must and will be regarded as the fine flower and crowning achievement of the genius and art of Bliss Carman.

R. H. HATHAWAY.
Toronto, 1921.

William Bliss Carman was born in Fredericton, in New Brunswick on April 15th 1861. 'Bliss' was his mother's maiden name. She was descended from Daniel Bliss of Concord, Massachusetts, who was the great-grandfather to Ralph Waldo Emerson.

Carman was educated at Fredericton Collegiate School. Here, under the influence of the headmaster George Robert Parkin, he gained an appreciation of classical literature and was introduced to the poetry of many of the Pre-Raphaelites especially Dante Gabriel Rossetti and Algernon Charles Swinburne.

From here he graduated to the University of New Brunswick, obtaining his B.A. there in 1881. As is common with so many writers his first published piece was for the University magazine and for Carman that was in 1879.

England now beckoned and he spent a year at Oxford and then the University of Edinburgh (1882–1883). He returned home to Canada to work on his M.A. which he obtained from the University of New Brunswick in 1884.

Tragically his father died in January, 1885, followed by his mother in February of the following year. Carman now enrolled in Harvard University for a year. There he met and was part of a literary circle that included the American poet Richard Hovey, who would become his close friend, and later collaborator, on the successful Vagabondia poetry series. Carman and Hovey were members of the "Visionists" circle along with Herbert Copeland and F. Holland Day, who would later form the Boston publishing firm Copeland & Day and, in turn, launch Vagabondia.

After Harvard Carman briefly returned to Canada, but was back in Boston by February of 1890 saying "Boston is one of the few places where my critical education and tastes could be of any use to me in earning money. New York and London are about the only other places." However, he was unable to find work in Boston but was more successful in New York becoming the literary editor of the semi-religious New York Independent. There he helped Canadian poets get published and introduced them to a wider readership than they could receive in Canada.

However, Carman and work as an editor were not destined for a long career together and he was dismissed in 1892. There followed short stays with Current Literature, Cosmopolitan, The Chap-Book, and The Atlantic Monthly. Whilst these appointments provided the basis for a career and an income he was not suited to their demands. From 1895 he would only work as a contributor to magazines and newspapers whilst he worked on his volumes of poetry.

Carman first published a book of poetry in 1893 with Low Tide on Grand Pré. He had written the title poem in the summer of 1886 and it had (whilst he was still at Harvard) been published in the spring of 1887 by Atlantic Monthly. Despite its critical acceptance there was no Canadian company prepared to publish the volume. When an American company did so it went bankrupt. Life was becoming difficult for the young poet.

The following year was decidedly better. His partnership with Richard Hovey had given birth to Songs of Vagabondia and it was published by their friends at Copeland & Day. It was an immediate success. The young men were delighted at such a reception. It quickly sold out and was re-printed a number of times. Although these re-prints were small (usually 500-1000 copies) they were frequent.

On the back of this success they would write a further three volumes, which in their turn were almost as successful. They quickly became the center of a cult following, especially among students who empathized with the poetry's anti-materialistic themes, its celebration of personal freedom, and its glorification of comradeship."

The success of Songs of Vagabondia prompted the Boston firm, Stone & Kimball, to reissue Low Tide on Grand Pré and to hire Carman as the editor of its literary journal, The Chapbook. This ceased after a year when the company relocated and Carman expressed his desire to remain in Boston.

In 1885 Carman brought out Behind the Arras, a somewhat more serious and philosophical work centered on the premise of a long meditation using the speaker's house and its many rooms as a symbol of life and the choices to be made. However, the idea and its execution did not quite meld.

Signficantly, in 1896, Carman met Mrs Mary Perry King, who rapidly became patron, adviser and sometime lover. She put money in his pocket, and food in his mouth and, when he struck bottom, often repaired his confidence as well as helping to sell the work. She also later became his writing collaborator on two verse dramas.

Mitchell Kennerley, Carman's roommate wrote that, "On the rare occasions they had intimate relations they always advised me of by leaving a bunch of violets — Mary favorite flower — on the pillow of my bed." If her husband, Dr. King, knew of this arrangement he seems not to have objected. He was a great supporter of Carman's career and seemingly his wife's complicated involvement with that.

In 1897 Carman published Ballad of Lost Haven, a collection of poetry about the sea. Its notable poems include the macabre sea shanty, The Gravedigger. The following year, 1898, came By the Aurelian Wall, the title poem itself was an elegy to John Keats and the book a collection of formal elegies.

In 1899 his publisher, Lamson, Wolffe was taken over by the Boston firm of Small, Maynard & Co., who had also acquired the rights to Low Tide on Grand Pré. The copyrights to of his books were now held by one publisher and, in lieu of earnings, Carman took what would ultimately be a disastrous financial stake in the company.

As the century turned Carman was hard at work on what would eventually be a five-volume set of poetry; "Pans Pipes". Pan, the goat-god, was traditionally associated with poetry and the coming together of the earthly and the divine. The five volumes were all published between 1902 – 1905.

The inspiration for this came from Mary who had persuaded Carman to write in both prose and poetry about the ideas of 'unitrinianism.' This drew on the theories of François-Alexandre-Nicolas-Chéri Delsarte and was defined as a strategy of mind-body-spirit harmonization aimed at undoing the physical, psychological, and spiritual damage caused by urban modernity. The definition may be rather woolly but for Carman it resulted in some very fine work across the five-volume series. This shared belief between Mary and Carman created a further bond but did isolate him from his circle of friends.

The excellence of a number of these poems did much to install Carman as the most noted of Canadian Poets and eventually their own Poet Laureate. Among the most often quoted and printed are "The Dead Faun" (from Volume I), "Lord of My Heart's Elation" (Volume II) and many of the erotic poems from Volume III.

In the middle of publication in 1903, Small, Maynard failed and with it went all the assets Carman had tied up in the company.

Carman immediately signed with another Boston publisher, L.C. Page, who would publish seven new books of Carman poetry in this hectic period up to 1905. They released a further three books based on Carman's Transcript columns, and a prose work on Unitrinianism, The Making of Personality, that he'd written with Mary King.

Carman now felt secure enough to pursue his 'dream project,' namely a deluxe edition of his collected poetry to 1903. Page acquired the distribution rights on the condition that the book be sold privately, by subscription. Unfortunately, the demand wasn't there and it failed. Carman was deeply disappointed and lost faith in Page. However, their grip on his copyrights was absolute and sadly no further collected editions were to be published during his lifetime.

By 1904 his income was restricted and the offer to be editor-in-chief of the 10-volume project, The World's Best Poetry, was eagerly accepted.

For Carman perhaps his best years as a poet were now behind him. From 1908 he lived near the Kings' New Canaan, Connecticut, estate, that he named "Sunshine", or in the summer in a cabin in the Catskills, which he called "Moonshine."

With Literary tastes now moving away from what he could provide his income further dwindled and his health started to deteriorate.

In 1912 Carman published the final work in the Vagabondia series. Richard Hovey had died in 1900 and so this last work was purely his. It has a distinct elegiac tone as if remembering the past works themselves.

Although Carman was not politically active he did campaign during the World War One, as a member of the Vigilantes, who supported the American entry into the titanic struggle on the Allied side.

By 1920, Carman was impoverished and recovering from a near-fatal attack of tuberculosis. He returned to Canada and began to undertake a series of publicly successful and somewhat lucrative reading tours, saying "there is nothing worth talking of in book sales compared with reading. Breathless attention, crowded halls, and a strange, profound enthusiasm such as I never guessed could be,' he reported to a friend. 'And good thrifty money too. Think of it! An entirely new life for me, and I am the most surprised person in Canada.'"

On October 28th, 1921 Carman was honored at a dinner held by the newly-formed Canadian Authors' Association, at the Ritz Carlton Hotel in Montreal, where he was crowned Canada's Poet Laureate with a wreath of maple leaves.

Carman is placed among the Confederation Poets, a group that included his cousin, Charles G.D. Roberts, Archibald Lampman, and Duncan Campbell Scott. Carman was perhaps the best and is credited with the widest recognition. However, whilst the others carefully supplemented their income with writing novels and works for the magazines, or even other careers, Carman only wrote poetry together with a small amount of writing on literary ideas, philosophy, and aesthetics.

He continued his reading tours, and by 1925 had finally secured a new Canadian publisher; McClelland & Stewart (Toronto), who issued a collection of selected earlier verse and would now became his main publisher. Although they benefited from Carman's increased popularity and his revered position in Canadian literature, his former publisher L.C. Page would not relinquish its copyrights to his earlier works.

In his last years, Carman was a member of the Halifax literary and social set, The Song Fishermen and in 1927 he edited The Oxford Book of American Verse.

William Bliss Carman died of a brain hemorrhage, at the age of 68, in New Canaan on the 8th June, 1929. He was cremated in New Canaan and his ashes interred at Forest Hill Cemetery, Fredericton, with a national memorial service held at the Anglican cathedral there.

It was only a quarter of a century later, on May 13th, 1954, that a scarlet maple tree was planted at his graveside, to honour his request in the 1892 poem "The Grave-Tree":

Let me have a scarlet maple
For the grave-tree at my head,
With the quiet sun behind it,
In the years when I am dead.

Bliss Carman – A Concise Bibliography

Poetry Collections
Low Tide on Grand Pre: A Book of Lyrics (1893)
Songs from Vagabondia (1894)
A Seamark: A Threnody for Robert Louis Stevenson (1895)
Behind the Arras: A Book of the Unseen (1895)
More Songs from Vagabondia (1896)
Ballads of Lost Haven: A Book of the Sea (1897)
By the Aurelian Wall: And Other Elegies (1898)
A Winter Holiday (1899)
Last Songs from Vagabondia (1901)
Ballads and Lyrics (1902)
Ode on the Coronation of King Edward (1902)
Pipes of Pan: From the Book of Myths (1902)
Pipes of Pan: From the Green Book of the Bards (1903)
Pipes of Pan: Songs of the Sea Children (1904)
Pipes of Pan: Songs from a Northern Garden (1904)
Pipes of Pan: From the Book of Valentines (1905)
Sappho: One Hundred Lyrics (1904)
Poems (1905)
The Rough Rider: And Other Poems (1909)
A Painter's Holiday, and Other Poems (1911)
Echoes from Vagabondia (1912)
April Airs: A Book of New England Lyrics (1916)
The Man of The Marne: And Other Poems (1918)
The Vengeance of Noel Brassard: A Tale of the Acadian Expulsion (1919)
Far Horizons (1925)
Later Poems (1926)
Sanctuary: Sunshine House Sonnets (1929)
Wild Garden (1929)
Bliss Carman's Poems (1931)

Drama

Bliss Carman & Mary Perry King. Daughters of Dawn: A Lyrical Pageant of a Series of Historical Scenes for Presentation with Music and Dancing (1913)

Bliss Carman & Mary Perry King. Earth Deities: And Other Rhythmic Masques (1914)

Prose Collections

The Kinship of Nature (1904)

The Poetry of Life (1905)

The Friendship of Art (1908)

The Making of Personality (1908)

Talks on Poetry and Life; Being a Series of Five Lectures Delivered Before the University of Toronto, December 1925 (Speech). transcribed by Blanche Hume. 1926.

Bliss Carman's Scrap-Book: A Table of Contents (Pierce, Lorne, editor) (1931)

Editor

The World's Best Poetry (10 volumes) (1904)

The Oxford Book of American Verse (U.S. editor) (1927)

Carman, Bliss; Pierce, Lorne, editors (1935). Our Canadian Literature: Representative Verse, English and French.

www.ingramcontent.com/pod-product-compliance
Lightning Source LLC
Chambersburg PA
CBHW060056050426
42448CB00011B/2485